Lincoln School Library

The Let's Talk Library™

Let's Talk About Drug Abuse

Anna Kreiner

The Rosen Publishing Group's

PowerKids Press™

New York

Published in 1996 by The Rosen Publishing Group, Inc.
29 East 21st Street, New York, NY 10010

First Edition

Book design: Erin McKenna

Photo credits: Cover and pp. 11, 16 by John Novajosky; p. 4 © Dusty Willison/International Stock; p. 7 by Michael Brandt; p. 8 © Peter Russell Clemens/International Stock; p. 12 by Michelle & Tom Grimm/International Stock; pp. 15, 20 by Lauren Piperno; p. 19 by Katie McClancy.

Kreiner, Anna.
    Let's talk about drug abuse /Anna Kreiner. — 1st ed.
        p.   cm. — (The Let's talk library)
    Includes index.
    Summary: A simple introduction to different drugs and how they affect the body and to the problem of drug abuse.
    ISBN 0-8239-2302-9
    1. Drug Abuse—Juvenile literature. 2. Drugs—Physiological effect—Juvenile literature. 3. Drugs of abuse—Juvenile literature. [1. Drugs. 2. Drug abuse.] I. Title. II. Series.
HV5809.5.K74 1996
362.29—dc20
                                                  95-48384
                                                    CIP
                                                      AC

Manufactured in the United States of America

Table of Contents

1   What Are Drugs?   5
2   Why Are Some Drugs Illegal?   6
3   Depressants   9
4   Hallucinogens   10
5   Narcotics   13
6   Why Do People Take Drugs?   14
7   When Someone Takes Drugs   17
8   Addiction   18
9   Drugs Hurt   21
10 Drugs and Your Friends   22
    Glossary   23
    Index   24

What Are Drugs?

Drugs are **chemicals** (KEM-ih-kulz) that change how you think and feel and act. Some drugs, like medicines, can help you. Your doctor or your parent may give you medicine like cough syrup or penicillin to help you get well when you are sick.

But some drugs can hurt you. Most of these drugs are **illegal** (il-LEE-gul). That means that it is against the law to buy, sell, or use them.

◀ *Medicines are drugs that can be good for you when used correctly.*

Why Are Some Drugs Illegal?

Some drugs are illegal because they hurt your body and your mind.

Stimulants (STIM-you-lents) like cocaine, crack, and **amphetamines** (am-FET-ah-meenz) make a person's body work faster. When someone takes a stimulant, his heart beats faster and he acts really wide awake. Taking stimulants can be dangerous because they can make a person's heart beat *too* fast. A person can die if his heart beats too fast too many times.

6

The drug crack speeds up and hurts a person's body. ▶

Depressants

Depressants, such as alcohol and **barbiturates** (bar-BICH-ur-rits), slow a person's body down. Alcohol is found in beer, wine, and liquor. It is legal for people who are 21 or older to drink alcohol. But if you drink alcohol before you are 21, you are breaking the law.

Barbiturates are pills that slow down a person's reactions and heart rate. It's not good for a person's heart to beat *too* slowly.

9

◀ *Alcohol slows a person's body down.*

Hallucinogens

Hallucinogens (hal-LOO-sin-uh-jens) make people see or hear things that aren't there or think things that aren't true. These drugs, such as **marijuana** (mare-ih-WA-na), LSD, and PCP, can cause people to do harmful things. A person who takes PCP may jump off a building because he thinks he can fly. A person who smokes marijuana may think that he doesn't have any problems, when really he is flunking out of school.

Some people smoke marijuana to forget about problems, but that doesn't solve them. ▶

Narcotics

Narcotics (nar-KOT-tiks) are drugs made from the seeds of flowers called poppies. These drugs, such as **heroin** (HARE-o-win) and China White, make pain go away. They also make a person very sleepy. A person who takes heroin doesn't feel very much. He doesn't care whether he eats, or sleeps, or goes to the bathroom. All that person cares about is getting more heroin.

◀ *Poppies are beautiful, but their seeds can be used to make drugs that are deadly.*

Why Do People Take Drugs?

People take drugs for many reasons. Some people take them because they want to try something new. Others take them to forget about problems in their lives. Still others take drugs because their friends do. They think that using drugs will make them cool or help them fit in. All drugs really do is hurt them.

When people take drugs that hurt them, they are **abusing** (a-BYOU-zing) drugs.

You don't have to take drugs just because your friends do. ▶

When Someone Takes Drugs

It is hard to tell how someone will act when he takes drugs. Depending on the drug a person takes, he may get very quiet and want to be alone. Or he may get angry and yell and throw things around. He may even try to hit other people. He may lie in bed all day. Or he may leave home for a while.

If you can, the best thing you can do when someone you know is taking drugs is stay away from him.

Some people get angry when they use drugs.

Addiction

One of the most dangerous parts of taking any drug is that a person could become **addicted** (uh-DIK-ted) to it. This means that his body now needs the drug, and feels sick without it. When someone feels like this, he is called an addict.

An addict usually does poorly at school or work. He may forget important days like birthdays and holidays. An addict loses control of many things in his life.

Addicts may have a hard time paying attention in school. ▶

Drugs Hurt

Different drugs cause different problems in a person's body. But all drugs cause the body to break down. When a person takes drugs, his body can't work the way it's supposed to. Some parts may even stop working. This may cause the person to get very sick. Sometimes people who take drugs even die.

◄ *Some drugs, such as stimulants, keep people from sleeping. This is harmful.*

Drugs and Your Friends

Someday one of your friends may offer *you* a drug. He may say it will be fun. Or that you're not cool if you don't try it. Or that he won't be your friend anymore.

If this happens, remember that drugs hurt you. Then ask yourself this: Would a real friend ask you to hurt yourself? Look the person in the eye and say, "No, thanks."

Glossary

abusing (a-BYOU-zing) Using something that hurts you.

addicted (uh-DIK-ted) Needing drugs to feel normal.

amphetamine (am-FET-ah-meen) One kind of stimulant.

barbiturate (bar-BICH-ur-rit) Depressant; drug that slows down your body.

chemical (KEM-ih-kul) Something that changes the way you think, feel, or act.

hallucinogen (hal-LOO-sin-uh-jen) Drug that makes you see or hear things that aren't really there.

heroin (HARE-o-win) Narcotic; drug made from the opium poppy.

illegal (il-LEE-gul) Against the law.

marijuana (mare-ih-WA-na) One kind of hallucinogen.

narcotic (nar-KOT-tik) Drug made from the opium poppy.

stimulant (STIM-you-lent) Drug that speeds up your body.

Index

A
abuse, drug, 14
  effects of, 5, 6,
      9, 10, 13,
      17, 18, 21
addiction, 18
alcohol, 9
amphetamines, 6

B
barbiturates, 9

C
chemicals, 5

China White, 13
cocaine, 6
crack, 6

D
depressants, 9
drugs, illegal, 5

H
hallucinogens, 10
heroin, 13

L
LSD, 10

M
marijuana, 10
medicine, 5

N
narcotics, 13

P
PCP, 10
pills, 9
poppies, 13

S
stimulants, 6